The Family Kitchen

SALADS

Contents

Published by Hinkler Books Pty Ltd
45–55 Fairchild Street
Heatherton Victoria 3202 Australia
www.hinkler.com.au

Text and images © Anthony Carroll 2010
Design and layout © Hinkler Books Pty Ltd 2013
Page layout: Dynamo Limited
Prepress: Splitting Image

ISBN: 978 1 7430 8332 1

Printed and bound in China

Introduction

Salads are a staple of our daily diets, served either at the start of meal, as an accompaniment or, in the French fashion, as a separate course before dessert. As the trend towards lighter eating continues, salads are increasingly popular as main meals, too, and there are several warm salads in this book that would be welcome at any time of the year.

Fresh fruits and vegetables offer a variety of tastes and textures and are packed with fibre and nutrients. The secret to a successful salad is simple:

- Always choose fresh, unblemished ingredients, then prepare them in an imaginative way.

- Salad leaves should be stored in a plastic food bag in the vegetable crisper section of your refrigerator. If necessary, separate leaves and wash just prior to using.

- Tomatoes should have a deep red colour and firm flesh. For the best flavour, bring them to room temperature before using.

- Continental (English) cucumbers should only be peeled if the skin is tough or bitter, as the skin is said to aid digestion.

- Watercress should be stored upright in the refrigerator in a container of water, and covered with a plastic food bag. Change the water daily to ensure lasting freshness.

- White and brown onions have a strong, pungent taste and should be used sparingly. The red onion is mild and sweet and adds a pretty colour to any salad. Spring onions, also known as scallions or green onions, give a mild, fresh onion flavour.

- Combine flavours carefully and always complement your salads with a suitable dressing or mayonnaise.

- Dress a green salad as close to serving time as possible – the longer the dressing sits on the leaves, the less crisp they will be.

Dressings

Basic Vinaigrette

Makes about 1 cup · Preparation 3 minutes

¾ cup olive oil

¼ cup cider vinegar

1 tablespoon Dijon mustard

freshly ground black pepper

1   Place oil, vinegar, mustard and black pepper to taste in a screw-top jar and shake well to combine. The foundation of many great salads where the freshness of the ingredients only need simple embellishment.

Herb Mayonnaise

Makes about 3 cups · Preparation 10 minutes

300ml (10fl oz) olive oil

300ml (10fl oz) grapeseed oil

2 cups fresh herbs of your choice, for example parsley, chives, basil, chervil

2 cloves garlic, peeled

2 eggs, plus 2 egg yolks

1 tablespoon Dijon mustard

1 tablespoon white wine vinegar

salt and freshly ground black pepper

1   Combine the olive and grapeseed oils and set aside. Process the herbs and garlic until chopped and set aside.

2   Place the eggs and egg yolks in a food processor and process for 2 minutes. While processing, add the mustard and half the vinegar and then add the oil mixture in a thin stream. When most of the oil has been used, stop the processor and add the herb mixture, remaining vinegar and remaining oil and process briefly to combine. Add salt and pepper to taste and chill until ready to use. Store in the refrigerator. Goes with everything.

Warm Shallot and Lemon Dressing

Makes approximately ¾ cup · Preparation and cooking 10 minutes

4 large French shallots

2 cloves garlic

3 tablespoons vegetable oil

juice of 2 lemons

zest of 1 lemon

3 tablespoons vegetable stock (broth)

salt and freshly ground black pepper

1 Peel and mince the shallots and garlic. Heat the oil in a small frying pan (skillet) until smoking, then add the shallots and garlic and sauté until translucent, about 5 minutes.

2 Whisk in the lemon juice, lemon zest and vegetable stock (broth). Add salt and pepper to taste and simmer briefly. Remove from the heat and allow to cool slightly before using.

Thousand Island Yoghurt Dressing

Makes about 1 cup · Preparation 5 minutes

2 tablespoons snipped fresh chives

¾ cup natural yoghurt

2 tablespoons white wine vinegar

2 tablespoons green olives, chopped

2 spring (green) onions, finely chopped

1 hard-boiled egg, chopped

1 tablespoon finely chopped green capsicum (pepper)

1 tablespoon tomato paste (purée)

½ teaspoon chilli sauce

1 Place all ingredients into a bowl and whisk to combine.

2 Store dressing in a screw-top jar in the refrigerator for up to 1 week.

Fish and Shellfish

Seafood is highly nutritious and makes a most attractive salad. The following recipes would be a perfect starter before a meaty main course, or on their own as a healthy light lunch.

Fijian Ceviche

Serves 4 · Preparation 5 minutes + 4 hours marinating

1¼kg (2½lb) firm white fish

1 cup fresh lime or lemon juice

300ml (10fl oz) canned coconut milk

salt and freshly ground black pepper

1 small red capsicum (pepper),
finely diced

1 small green capsicum (pepper),
finely diced

1 small red chilli, minced

1 firm tomato, finely diced

lime or lemon wedges

1 Cut the fish into 12mm (½ in) cubes and mix with 200ml (7fl oz) of the lime juice, half the coconut milk, and salt and pepper to taste. Stir well and marinate for 4 hours.

2 When the fish is firm and looks opaque (cooked), drain away and discard the liquid.

3 Mix the drained fish with the capsicum (pepper) pieces, chilli and tomato. Add the remaining coconut milk and lime juice and stir to combine thoroughly.

4 Serve cold in glasses with wedges of lime or lemon as an entrée.

Marinated Salmon, Cucumber and Daikon Salad

Serves 6 · Preparation 20 minutes + 2 hours marinating

700g (1½lb) fillet of salmon, centre-cut

6 tablespoons mirin (sweet Japanese rice wine)

3 tablespoons Japanese soy sauce

5cm (2in) piece ginger (gingerroot), grated

1 teaspoon toasted sesame oil

1 continental (English) cucumber

1 teaspoon sea salt

1 tablespoon caster (berry) sugar

3 tablespoons rice vinegar

curly endive (chicory), well washed and dried

1 daikon (white radish), finely julienned

1 Ask your fishmonger to slice the salmon thinly, as for smoked salmon. If they can't or won't, have the skin removed and slice the salmon into very thin strips – if you feel you are able to slice the salmon on an angle this would be desirable, but if not, cut straight down.

2 Whisk the mirin, soy, ginger (gingerroot) and sesame oil together, then remove 2 tablespoons and reserve. Pour the remainder into a shallow bowl and add the sliced salmon fillet, allowing the fish to marinate for 2 hours.

3 Meanwhile, peel the cucumber and, using a vegetable peeler or food slicer, cut the cucumber into long, thin slices and place these in a bowl. Mix together the sea salt, sugar and rice vinegar and drizzle over the cucumber, tossing well to coat the slices in the dressing.

4 Arrange slices of marinated salmon on the plates then place the curly endive (chicory) and daikon (white radish) in the centre. Weave some drained cucumber slices through the salad then drizzle a little of the reserved mirin dressing over the salad.

Prawn and Avocado Cocktail

Serves 4 · Preparation 15 minutes

400g (14oz) cooked peeled prawns
(shrimp), defrosted if frozen

8 tablespoons mayonnaise

4 tablespoons tomato sauce (ketchup)

2 stalks (ribs) celery, finely chopped

1 spring (green) onion, finely sliced

salt and freshly ground black pepper

2 avocados

1 tablespoon lemon juice

1 Mix together the prawns (shrimp),
mayonnaise and tomato sauce (ketchup) in
a bowl, then stir in the celery and onion and
season to taste.

2 Halve the avocados, remove the stones
and peel. Dice the flesh, then toss in the
lemon juice to stop it browning. Add to the
prawn mixture, stirring lightly, then transfer
to glasses or serving plates and grind over a
little extra pepper.

Garlic Prawn Salad

Serves 4 · Preparation and cooking 16 minutes

1 tablespoon extra virgin olive oil

4 cloves garlic, crushed

½ teaspoon chilli flakes

24 large raw prawns (shrimp), shelled and deveined

1 medium tomato, sliced

1 cos (romaine) lettuce, outer leaves discarded

1 Lebanese or continental (English) cucumber, sliced into ribbons

salt and freshly ground black pepper

juice of 1 lime

juice of 1 lemon

1 Heat a large heavy-based frying pan (skillet), add the oil, garlic, chilli flakes and prawns (shrimp). Cook, stirring constantly, until the prawns change colour, about 3 minutes.

2 Divide the tomato slices between 4 serving plates, top with lettuce leaves and cucumber ribbons. Add the prawns and pour over the pan juices. Season with salt and pepper, then squeeze over the lemon and lime juices and serve.

Mixed Shellfish and Potato Salad

Serves 4 · Preparation and cooking 1 hour 15 minutes

750g (1½lb) waxy potatoes, unpeeled

4 small cooked beetroots, diced

1 bulb fennel, finely sliced, plus feathery top, chopped

1kg (2lb) mussels

500g (1lb) clams

300ml (10fl oz) dry white wine or cider

1 French shallot, finely chopped

4 spring (green) onions, finely sliced

¼ cup fresh parsley, chopped

Dressing

75ml (2½fl oz) olive oil

1 tablespoon cider vinegar

1 teaspoon English mustard

salt and freshly ground black pepper

1 Boil the potatoes in salted water for 15 minutes or until tender, then drain. Cool for 30 minutes, then peel and slice.

2 Meanwhile, make the dressing by whisking together the oil, vinegar, mustard and seasoning.

3 Place the potatoes in a bowl and toss with half the dressing. Toss the beetroots and fennel with the rest of the dressing.

4 Scrub the mussels and clams under cold running water, pulling away any beards from the mussels. Discard any shellfish that are open or damaged. Place the wine or cider and French shallot in a large saucepan and bring to the boil. Simmer for 2 minutes, then add the shellfish. Cover and cook briskly for 3–5 minutes, shaking the pan often, until the shellfish have opened. Discard any that remain closed. Reserve the pan juices, set aside a few mussels in their shells and shell the rest.

5 Boil the pan juices for 5 minutes or until reduced to 15–25ml (½–1fl oz). Strain over the potatoes. Add the shellfish flesh, spring (green) onions and parsley, then toss. Serve with the beetroot and fennel salad and garnish with the fennel tops and reserved mussels in their shells.

Tuna Barley Niçoise

Serves 6 · Preparation and cooking 1 hour 45 minutes

2 pink potatoes, unpeeled

1 teaspoon olive oil

salt and freshly ground black pepper

2 fresh rosemary sprigs, leaves removed and chopped

1 litre (35fl oz) mild vegetable stock (broth)

1 teaspoon fresh oregano

1 teaspoon fresh marjoram

1 cup pearl barley

1 red onion, sliced into rings

6 tuna steaks, about 180g (6½oz) each

500g (1lb) green (string) beans, blanched

½ cup fresh parsley, chopped

120g (4oz) mixed salad leaves

200g (7oz) roasted capsicum (pepper), sliced

2 Roma tomatoes, finely chopped

150g (5oz) Kalamata olives, finely chopped

Dressing

4 cloves garlic, minced

1 teaspoon mixed dried herbs

1–2 tablespoons virgin olive oil

1 teaspoon Dijon mustard

½ cup vegetable stock (broth)

1 Preheat oven to 220ºC (200ºC fan, 430ºF, gas 7). Wash the potatoes well and slice (do not peel). Brush lightly or spray with olive oil. Sprinkle with salt, pepper and rosemary and bake on a baking tray (sheet) for 45 minutes, turning during the cooking time.

2 Meanwhile, bring the stock (broth) to a boil and add the oregano and marjoram. Add the barley, cover and simmer for 40 minutes. Remove from heat and set aside. Soak the red onion in cold water for 30 minutes, then drain.

3 Season the tuna steaks with salt and pepper and cook on a preheated grill (broil) pan for 2 minutes each side, until just cooked.

4 To make the dressing, whisk together all ingredients until thick, then set aside. Mix green (string) beans, onions rings, parsley and half the dressing with the warm barley and toss thoroughly to distribute.

5 To assemble, place several slices of potato on the centre of each plate, top with 6 salad leaves, a generous spoonful of barley mixture, some roasted capsicum (pepper) and a cooked tuna steak. Place teaspoonsful of finely chopped tomato and olives around the salad, then drizzle everything with remaining dressing. Sprinkle with extra parsley and serve at room temperature.

Meat and Poultry

A hearty salad can be a meal in itself. One-dish recipes such as Indian Salad of Spiced Chicken and Dhal or Warm Duck and Mango Salad offer a contrast in textures and temperatures and are suitable for any season.

Asian Chicken Bok Choy Salad

Serves 6–8 · Preparation and soaking 40 minutes

8 fresh or dried shiitake mushrooms

10g (¼oz) black cloud ear fungus

800g (28oz) cooked chicken, skin off, shredded

1kg (2lb) fresh Asian noodles

200g (7oz) fresh snow peas (mange tout), diagonally sliced

4 baby bok choy, well washed and leaves separated

1 red capsicum (pepper), diced

4 spring (green) onions, finely sliced

250g (8oz) canned sliced water chestnuts, drained

4cm (2in) piece fresh ginger (gingerroot), minced

¼ cup natural yoghurt

3 tablespoons kecap (ketjap) manis

1 tablespoon hoisin sauce

3 tablespoons mirin

3 tablespoons rice vinegar

3 tablespoons sweet-chilli sauce

1 tablespoon fish sauce

juice of 1 lime

salt and freshly ground black pepper

2 tablespoons slivered almonds, toasted

1 bunch chervil, parsley or coriander (cilantro)

1 If using dried shiitake, soak in hot water for 15 minutes then drain and slice. If using fresh shiitake, slice finely. Soak the black cloud ear fungus for 15 minutes then drain. Rinse the soaked mushrooms thoroughly in cold water.

2 Place the shredded cooked chicken in a large bowl. Pour boiling hot water over the noodles until they have separated, then shake off excess water and add the noodles to the chicken. Add the mushrooms, snow peas (mange tout), baby bok choy leaves, capsicum (pepper), spring (green) onions and water chestnuts and toss well.

3 In a jug, whisk together the ginger (gingerroot), yoghurt, kecap (ketjap) manis, hoisin, mirin, rice vinegar, sweet-chilli sauce, fish sauce, lime juice and salt and pepper to taste. Add to the chicken salad and toss very well until all the ingredients are coated. Garnish with the toasted slivered almonds and chopped chervil, parsley or coriander (cilantro) and serve.

Israeli Kumquat Chicken Salad with Mixed Wild Rice

Serves 6–8 · Preparation and cooking 40 minutes + 2 hours marinating

1kg (2lb) lean chicken, diced

1 teaspoon freshly ground black salt

1 teaspoon pepper

1 teaspoon paprika

1 teaspoon ground cumin

1 teaspoon onion powder

2 cups orange juice

¼ cup dry white wine

2 onions, diced

4 tablespoons apricot jam (jelly)

4 tablespoons peach jam (jelly)

4 tablespoons honey

2 tablespoons lemon juice

2 tablespoons lime juice

500g (1lb) fresh or canned kumquat

¼ cup wild rice

½ cup brown rice

1 cup white rice

1 bunch basil, leaves thinly sliced

100g (3½oz) toasted pistachio nuts, chopped

1 Place the diced chicken in a plastic bag and add the salt, pepper, paprika, ground cumin and onion powder and seal the bag. Shake vigorously to coat the chicken with the spice mix then thread the spiced chicken pieces onto wooden skewers and place them in a shallow baking dish. Set aside.

2 Meanwhile mix the orange juice, wine, onions, both jams (jellies), honey, lemon juice, lime juice and kumquats in a saucepan and heat until just about to boil. Pour half this mixture (reserving the remaining mixture) over the chicken skewers and marinate for 2 hours.

3 While the chicken is marinating, prepare the rice. Bring a large pot of salted water to the boil and add the wild rice. Boil for 5 minutes then add the brown rice. Boil these together for a further 10 minutes before adding the white rice and simmering for 15 minutes. Drain thoroughly and keep warm.

4 Heat a frying pan (skillet), barbecue or griller (broiler) and cook the chicken skewers until cooked through, brushing them with the remaining kumquat mixture as they cook.

5 Fold the finely sliced fresh basil and chopped pistachio nuts through the rice then serve with the chicken skewers. Drizzle any remaining kumquat mixture over if desired.

Italian Sausage Salad with Mizuna Leaves

Serves 4 · Preparation and cooking 40 minutes

2 medium zucchini (courgettes), cut into 1cm (½in) slices

350g (12oz) Italian sausages

1 thin baguette, cut into 2cm (1in) slices

2 tablespoons olive oil

2 bunches mizuna leaves

¼ cup basil leaves, shredded

125g (4oz) sundried tomatoes

45g (1½oz) parmesan cheese, grated

Dressing

¼ cup olive oil

2 tablespoons lemon juice

salt and freshly ground black pepper

1 Lightly brush a chargrill (char-broil) pan with oil, and heat. Chargrill zucchini (courgettes) for 2–3 minutes each side, then remove and set aside.

2 Add the sausages to the grill and cook for 6–8 minutes, turning frequently, then remove and set aside to cool. When cool, slice sausages into 25mm (1in) slices.

3 Brush slices of bread with the oil, and cook on chargrill for 2–3 minutes each side. Combine mizuna leaves, basil, sausages, zucchini, sundried tomatoes and parmesan in a large bowl.

4 To make the dressing, mix together oil, lemon juice, salt and pepper, and whisk. Drizzle dressing over salad before serving.

Indian Salad of Spiced Chicken and Dhal

Serves 6–8 · Preparation and cooking 50 minutes

7½ cups vegetable stock (broth)

1½ cups dried lentils

juice of 2 lemons

2 tablespoons vegetable oil

1 tablespoon curry powder
(jerk seasoning)

1 tablespoon garam masala

1 teaspoon turmeric

salt and freshly ground black pepper

4 large chicken breast fillets,
skin removed

1 small cauliflower, cut into florets

1½ cups fresh or frozen peas

2 small tomatoes, deseeded and diced

1 continental (English) cucumber, peeled
and diced

2 spring (green) onions, sliced

¼ cup fresh mint, chopped

2 large bunches watercress, trimmed

1 Bring 6 cups of vegetable stock (broth) to the boil and add the lentils. Simmer until the lentils are tender but still retain their shape, about 20 minutes. Drain well then transfer the lentils to a large bowl and add the lemon juice and 1 tablespoon of the oil. Mix well, cover and chill.

2 Combine the curry powder (jerk seasoning), garam masala and turmeric in a plastic bag with salt and pepper to taste then add the chicken breasts to the bag. Seal the bag and shake vigorously, allowing the spices to coat the chicken breasts evenly. Heat a grill (broil) pan or non-stick frying pan (skillet) with the remaining oil until smoking then add the chicken breasts to the pan and cook until cooked through and golden brown on both sides. Remove the chicken and set aside.

3 To the same pan, add the remaining stock and bring to the boil. Add the cauliflower and peas and cook over high heat until vegetables are crisp-tender and most of liquid has evaporated, about 5 minutes. Add this vegetable mixture to the lentils and mix well. Add the tomatoes, cucumber, spring (green) onions and fresh mint and mix well, adding more salt and pepper to taste.

4 Slice the chicken into diagonal strips then gently mix these into the salad. Arrange the watercress on a platter and top with the salad mixture, arranging so that there is plenty of chicken visible. Garnish with extra mint.

Tandoori Lamb Salad
with Black Onion

Serves 6 · Preparation and cooking 25 minutes plus 4–8 hours marinating

12 large lamb cutlets

1 cup sesame seeds

½ cup black onion seeds

Marinade

1 large onion, chopped

25mm (1in) piece fresh ginger
(gingerroot), grated

juice of 1 lemon

½ cup plain yoghurt

2 teaspoons ground coriander

2 teaspoons ground cumin

½ teaspoon ground turmeric

¼ teaspoon cayenne pepper

1 tablespoon garam masala

¼ teaspoon nutmeg (mace)

1 teaspoon salt

Salad

250g (8oz) baby spinach leaves

200g (7oz) mixed baby lettuce leaves

4 spring (green) onions, sliced

2 tablespoons white vinegar

3 tablespoons peanut oil

salt and freshly ground black pepper

few drops of toasted sesame oil

1   To make the marinade, place the onion, ginger (gingerroot), lemon juice and 1 tablespoon water in a food processor with the yoghurt, spices and salt and process until the mixture is smooth. Remove from the processor and pour over the lamb cutlets, turning to coat both sides of the lamb. Marinate for a minimum of 4 hours or up to 8 hours.

2   Preheat the oven to 220ºC (200ºC fan, 430ºF, gas 7). When you are ready to cook, mix the sesame seeds and onion seeds together and place them on a plate. Remove the lamb cutlets from the marinade one at a time, allowing the excess to run off, then dip each cutlet in the sesame mixture, coating both sides. Place the coated cutlets on a non-stick baking tray (sheet) and bake in the preheated oven for 10 minutes for medium rare, or longer if you prefer.

3   Meanwhile, prepare the salad. Wash and dry the spinach and mixed lettuce leaves and place them, with the spring (green) onions, in a large salad bowl. Whisk together the vinegar and peanut oil with salt and pepper to taste then add the few drops of sesame oil, continuing to whisk until the dressing is thick. Toss the salad with the dressing until the leaves are well coated then divide the salad between 6 plates. Arrange 2 cutlets on each plate and serve immediately.

Salad of Sautéed Duck with Thyme and Honey

Serves 4 · Preparation and cooking 45 minutes

3 duck breasts, skin on

salt and freshly ground black pepper

1 tablespoon peanut oil

2 teaspoons butter

2 sprigs thyme

2 tablespoons honey

1 tablespoon lemon juice

2 tablespoons walnut oil

200g (7oz) mixed baby lettuce leaves, washed and spun dry

6 large cherry tomatoes

¼ cup basil leaves

1 Heat the oven to 190ºC (170ºC fan, 375ºF, gas 5). Season each duck breast with a little salt and pepper.

2 Heat peanut oil in a pan until almost smoking then add the duck breasts, skin-side down, and cook on a high heat until the skin is deep caramel brown. Transfer the pan containing the duck to the preheated oven until the duck is cooked rare, about 7–10 minutes. Do not turn the duck breasts over.

3 Remove the pan from the oven and remove the breasts from pan, keeping them warm, and drain and discard the excess fat. Add the butter, and when it begins to bubble, add the thyme then the honey. When simmering, replace duck breasts, skin-side up.

4 Cook for a further minute on low heat then remove from the pan altogether.

5 Whisk together the lemon juice, walnut oil, salt and pepper and the pan juices and mix well. Toss the lettuce leaves through a little of the dressing.

6 Divide the lettuce leaves between the plates, garnish with tomatoes. Slice duck breast and arrange around the salad, drizzling any excess honey sauce over the duck slices. Garnish with basil leaves and serve.

Summer Salad of Chicken, Spinach and Mango

Serves 6 · Preparation and cooking 2 hours 20 minutes + 1–4 hours marinating

6 Roma tomatoes

10 basil leaves, sliced

10 mint leaves, sliced

salt and freshly ground black pepper

½ teaspoon white (granulated) sugar

12 chicken tenderloins

1 bunch asparagus

1 avocado

1 bunch spring (green) onions

8 firm button mushrooms

2 firm mangoes

3 handfuls baby spinach leaves

½ cup toasted hazelnuts, lightly crushed

½ cup toasted Brazil nuts, lightly crushed

½ cup toasted pistachios, lightly crushed

Dressing

2 teaspoons honey

2 tablespoons balsamic vinegar

3 tablespoons raspberry vinegar

2 tablespoons soy sauce

2 teaspoons Dijon mustard

25mm (1in) piece ginger (gingerroot), minced

2 cloves garlic, minced

1 teaspoon sambal oelek (chilli paste)

2 tablespoons lemon juice

2 tablespoons olive oil

salt and freshly ground black pepper

1 Preheat the oven to 160°C (140°C fan, 320°F, gas 3). Slice the tomatoes in half lengthwise, and top with sliced basil, mint, salt, pepper and sugar. Bake for 2 hours, then cut into quarters.

2 In a large jug, whisk together all the dressing ingredients until emulsified (thickened).

3 Marinate the chicken in ½ cup of dressing, reserving the remainder for later. Allow the chicken to marinate for 1 hour minimum (or up to 4 hours). Heat a non-stick grill (broil) pan and cook the chicken over a high heat until cooked through, 2–3 minutes on each side. Transfer the cooked chicken to a plate and keep warm.

4 Steam the asparagus until tender then refresh under cold water. Halve the avocado, peel and dice the flesh. Slice the spring (green) onions diagonally and thinly slice the mushrooms. Dice the mango flesh.

5 To make the salad, place the well-washed spinach leaves in a large bowl and add the asparagus, spring onions, mushrooms and roasted tomatoes. Add the reserved dressing and toss thoroughly.

6 Divide the salad evenly amongst six individual plates and add the mango and avocado cubes. Top each with 2 chicken tenderloins, and a generous sprinkling of nuts. Serve immediately.

Warm Duck and Mango Salad

Serves 4 · Preparation and cooking 35 minutes

250g (8oz) boneless duck breast

2 teaspoons sesame oil

1 ripe mango

125g (4oz) mixed dark salad leaves, such as baby spinach and rocket (arugula)

125g (4oz) snow peas (mange tout), chopped

4 spring (green) onions, sliced diagonally

Dressing

3 tablespoons extra virgin olive oil

juice of 1 lime

1 teaspoon clear honey

¼ cup fresh coriander (cilantro), chopped

freshly ground black pepper

1 Skin the duck breasts and cut into strips. Heat the sesame oil in a wok or large frying pan (skillet), add the duck and stir-fry (scramble-fry) over a high heat for 4–5 minutes until tender.

2 Slice off the 2 fat sides of the mango close to the stone. Cut a criss-cross pattern across the flesh (but not the skin) of each side with a sharp knife. Push the skin inside out to expose the flesh and cut the cubes off. Place in a salad bowl with the salad leaves, snow peas (mange tout) and spring (green) onions, then toss together gently to mix.

3 To make the dressing, whisk together the olive oil, lime juice, honey, coriander (cilantro) and black pepper in a small bowl until thoroughly mixed. Add the warm duck to the mango salad, drizzle over the dressing, then toss together to mix. Garnish with fresh coriander.

Grains, Pulses and Pasta

Grains, pulses and pasta form the basis of many satisfying salads. Combined with fresh vegetables, herbs and spices they can be a nutritious light meal or a filling side dish.

Japanese Rice Noodle Salad

Serves 2 · Preparation and cooking 35 minutes

250g (8oz) long, flat rice noodles

1 teaspoon olive oil

25mm (1in) piece ginger (gingerroot), grated

1–2 small fresh red chillies, deseeded and minced

1 red capsicum (pepper), cut into small chunks

6 spring (green) onions, sliced on the diagonal

½ bunch coriander (cilantro)

juice of 1 lime

1 tablespoon Japanese rice vinegar

1 tablespoon soy sauce

2 tablespoons vegetable stock (broth)

3 tablespoons sesame seeds

1 Fill a large jug or bowl with hot (not boiling) water and immerse the rice noodles, allowing them to soak until soft, about 5–10 minutes. Drain and rinse under cold water to refresh them, then place the noodles in a large mixing bowl.

2 Heat the olive oil in a small non-stick pan and add the ginger (gingerroot) and chillies and sauté gently for 1–2 minutes. Add the chopped capsicum (pepper) pieces, raise the heat to medium-high and stir-fry (scramble-fry) until the capsicum pieces are softened. Add the spring (green) onion slices and continue to cook for a further 2 minutes.

3 Tip the capsicum mixture into the mixing bowl with the noodles and add the coriander (cilantro), tossing thoroughly.

4 In a small jug, whisk together the lime juice, rice vinegar, soy and stock (broth) and toss through the noodles. Sprinkle with the sesame seeds and chill before serving.

Turkish Tabouli

Serves 4 · Preparation and cooking 1 hour 40 minutes + 2 hours chilling

¾ cup fine bulgar wheat

½ bunch spring (green) onions, trimmed and finely sliced

1 large ripe tomato, deseeded and diced

½ red capsicum (pepper), deseeded and diced

1 small continental (English) cucumber, peeled, deseeded and diced

1 cup parsley, finely chopped

¼ cup fresh mint, sliced

2 tablespoons Turkish red capsicum (pepper) paste (see below)

juice of 1 lemon

3 tablespoons olive oil

½ tablespoon pomegranate molasses

2 teaspoons ground cumin

salt and freshly ground black pepper

Turkish red capsicum (pepper) paste

2 red capsicums (peppers), flesh only

2 hot red chillies

½ teaspoon salt

½ teaspoon white (granulated) sugar

2 teaspoons olive oil

1 To make the Turkish red capsicum (pepper) paste, place the capsicums, chillies, salt, sugar and olive oil in a food processor with 1 tablespoon water and process until smooth. Transfer the mixture to a saucepan and simmer gently until the mixture is thick and the liquid has reduced, about 1 hour, stirring frequently. Cool.

2 Cover the bulgar with cool water and allow to stand for 30 minutes. Drain well, squeezing out any excess water. In a mixing bowl, combine the bulgar, spring (green) onions, tomato, capsicum, cucumber, parsley and mint and mix well. Add the red capsicum paste and mix thoroughly until the salad takes on a lovely red hue.

3 Whisk together the lemon juice, olive oil, pomegranate molasses, cumin and salt and pepper. Pour the dressing over the vegetable mixture and toss thoroughly to make sure all the ingredients are coated. Add extra salt to taste, if necessary, then chill for 2 hours. Serve cold or at room temperature.

Greek Orzo Salad with Olives

Serves 4 · Preparation and cooking 1 hour

350g (12oz) orzo or rice-shaped pasta

170g (6oz) fetta cheese, crumbled

1 red capsicum (pepper), finely chopped

1 yellow capsicum (pepper),
finely chopped

1 green capsicum (pepper), finely chopped

170g (6oz) pitted Kalamata
olives, chopped

4 spring (green) onions, sliced

2 tablespoons drained capers

3 tablespoons pine nuts, toasted

Dressing

2 lemons, juice and zest

1 tablespoon white wine vinegar

4 large cloves garlic, minced

1½ teaspoons dried oregano

1 teaspoon Dijon mustard

1 teaspoon ground cumin

100ml (3½fl oz) olive oil

1 Cook the orzo in a large pot of boiling salted water until tender but still firm to bite. Drain and rinse with cold water then place in a large bowl with a little olive oil.

2 Add the fetta, capsicums (peppers), olives, spring (green) onions and capers.

3 To make the dressing, whisk together the lemon juice and zest, vinegar, garlic, oregano, mustard and cumin in a small bowl. Gradually add the olive oil, then season to taste with salt and pepper.

4 Drizzle the dressing over the salad and toss thoroughly. Garnish with the toasted pine nuts and serve.

Fragrant Indian Salad

Serves 8 · Preparation and cooking 30 minutes + 2 hours standing

2 cups dried chickpeas (garbanzo beans)

4 onions

1 teaspoon whole cloves

4 bay leaves

¼ cup peanut or olive oil

4 cloves garlic, minced

1 teaspoon ground turmeric

2 teaspoons ground cumin

2 teaspoons garam masala

3 tablespoons tomato paste (purée)

2 red capsicums (peppers), sliced

4 medium zucchini (courgettes), sliced on the diagonal

salt and freshly ground black pepper

500g (1lb) baby spinach

1 Pick over the chickpeas (garbanzo beans) and remove any that are discoloured. Place all remaining chickpeas in a large saucepan and cover with cold water. Peel 2 of the onions and chop in half. Place these in the saucepan with the chickpeas. Add the cloves and bay leaves, bring to the boil and simmer for 10 minutes, then remove the chickpeas from the heat, cover and allow to stand for 2 hours. Strain the chickpeas, discarding the onions, cloves and bay leaves, but reserving the soaking water.

2 Meanwhile, chop the remaining 2 onions. Heat the oil and sauté the onions and the minced garlic. Add all the spices and cook briefly to release their fragrance. Add the soaked chickpeas and 2 cups of the soaking water, the tomato paste (purée) and the red capsicum (pepper) strips.

3 Cover and simmer gently for about 20 minutes until the chickpeas soften and the liquid evaporates. Add the zucchini (courgettes) and salt and pepper to taste, stir well then remove from the heat. Allow to cool slightly then fold through the spinach leaves.

4 Cool completely and serve.

Spicy Wild Rice Salad

Serves 4 · Preparation and cooking 40 minutes

400g (14oz) wild rice blend (brown and wild rice mix)

2 tablespoons vegetable oil

2 onions, cut into thin wedges

1 teaspoon ground cumin

½ teaspoon ground cinnamon

¼ teaspoon ground cloves

¼ teaspoon ground ginger

2 carrots, thinly sliced

1 teaspoon honey

2 oranges, segmented

90g (3oz) raisins (dark raisins)

90g (3oz) pistachios, toasted and roughly chopped

60g (2oz) flaked almonds, toasted

3 spring (green) onions, sliced

10 sprigs fresh dill (dill weed), chopped

Dressing

1 teaspoon Dijon mustard

½ cup olive oil

¼ cup orange juice

1 tablespoon red wine vinegar

1 Combine the rice with 3½ cups water in a saucepan. Bring to the boil, reduce heat to low, cover and cook for 15 minutes. Remove pan from heat, allow to stand covered for 10 minutes. Drain well and set aside to cool.

2 Heat oil in a non-stick frying pan (skillet) over a medium heat, add onions, cumin, cinnamon, cloves and ginger and cook, stirring, for 10 minutes or until onions are soft and slightly caramelised. Add carrots and cook until tender. Stir in honey, then remove from heat and cool slightly.

3 Place rice, carrot mixture, oranges, raisins, pistachios, almonds, spring (green) onions and dill (dill weed) in a bowl and toss to combine.

4 To make dressing, place mustard, oil, orange juice and vinegar in a bowl and whisk to combine. Pour dressing over salad and toss.

Bulgar Wheat Salad

Serves 4 · Preparation and cooking 35 minutes + 20 minutes soaking

250g (8oz) bulgar wheat

2 yellow capsicums (peppers), quartered and deseeded

250g (8oz) green (string) beans, halved

2 ripe tomatoes

4 spring (green) onions, sliced

90g (3oz) Brazil nuts, roughly chopped

½ cup fresh parsley, chopped

sea salt and freshly ground black pepper

Dressing

4 tablespoons extra virgin olive oil

1 tablespoon wholegrain mustard

1 clove garlic, crushed

1 teaspoon balsamic vinegar

1 teaspoon white wine vinegar

1 Place the bulgar in a bowl and cover with boiling water to about 2cm (¾in) above the level of the bulgar and leave to soak for 20 minutes. Meanwhile, preheat the griller (broiler) to high. Grill (broil) the capsicums (peppers), skin-side up, for 15–20 minutes until the skin is blistered and blackened all over. Transfer to a plastic bag, seal and leave to cool. When cold enough to handle, remove and discard the charred skins and roughly chop the flesh.

2 Blanch the beans in boiling water for 3–4 minutes, drain, refresh under cold running water and set aside. Put the tomatoes into a bowl, cover with boiling water and leave for 30 seconds. Peel, deseed, then roughly chop the flesh.

3 Combine the ingredients for the dressing and mix well. Drain the bulgar and transfer to a salad bowl. Add the dressing and toss well. Add the vegetables, spring (green) onions, Brazil nuts, parsley and seasoning and toss together gently to mix.

South American Bean Salad

Serves 4 · Preparation 18 minutes

800g (1½lb) canned cannellini (haricot) beans, drained and rinsed

1 small red onion, thinly sliced

1 small red capsicum (pepper), roasted and thinly sliced

1 jalapeño chilli, deseeded and diced

3 cups watercress sprigs, washed

¼ cup flat-leaf parsley leaves

2 tablespoons extra virgin olive oil

1 tablespoon lemon juice

2 tablespoons red wine vinegar

½ teaspoon white (granulated) sugar

salt and freshly ground black pepper

1 Place beans in a serving bowl. Add red onion, red capsicum (pepper), chilli, watercress and parsley.

2 Combine olive oil, lemon juice, red wine vinegar, sugar, salt and pepper in a small bowl.

3 Pour dressing over and toss to combine.

Warm Mediterranean Pasta Shell Salad

Serves 4 · Preparation and cooking 30 minutes

175g (6oz) dried pasta shells

150g (5oz) fine green (string) beans, halved

4 spring (green) onions, sliced

1 green capsicum (pepper), deseeded and chopped

125g (4oz) cherry tomatoes, halved

1 large ripe avocado, chopped

freshly ground black pepper

2 sprigs fresh basil leaves, torn

Dressing

3 tablespoons olive or sunflower oil

1 tablespoon white wine vinegar

1 tablespoon clear honey

1 teaspoon Dijon mustard

1 To make the dressing, place the oil, vinegar, honey and mustard in a screw-top jar and shake well to combine.

2 Bring a large saucepan of salted water to the boil, add the pasta and cook for 6 minutes. Add the green (string) beans and cook for 2 minutes or until the pasta is tender but still firm to the bite (al dente) and the beans have softened. Drain well.

3 Place the pasta and beans in a large bowl with the spring (green) onions, green capsicum (pepper), cherry tomatoes, avocado and seasoning. Add the dressing and toss well. Garnish with the basil.

Barley, Fetta and Pear Salad

Serves 6 · Preparation and cooking 40 minutes

1 cup pearl barley

½ cup walnuts

1 cup fresh flat-leaf parsley leaves

3 stalks (ribs) celery

1–2 firm ripe pears

100g (3½oz) fresh rocket (arugula) leaves

100g (3½oz) crumbled fetta

juice of 1 lemon

3 tablespoons extra virgin olive oil

salt and freshly ground black pepper

1 Place the barley in a large saucepan, partially cover with hot water and boil until tender, about 30 minutes.

2 While barley is cooking, toast walnuts in a small frying pan (skillet) until golden and fragrant. Set aside.

3 Chop the parsley and cut celery into fine slices. Peel and core pear and cut into fine wedges then mix with the rocket (arugula), parsley and celery.

4 Drain barley in a sieve and transfer to a bowl. Add fetta and nuts and mix well. Add the rocket mixture.

5 Whisk the lemon juice, oil, salt and pepper then toss through salad until combined.

Vegetables

Vegetable salads make healthy and colourful side dishes, adding a wide range of tastes and textures to meats, poultry, fish, omelettes and quiches.

Tuscan Panzanella with Roasted Tomato Vinaigrette

Serves 4 · Preparation and cooking 45 minutes

300g (10oz) stale, rustic Italian-style bread

2 tablespoons olive oil

2 sprigs fresh rosemary, leaves removed and chopped

500g (1lb) assorted tomatoes

1 continental (English) cucumber

10 Kalamata olives

1 small red onion, finely chopped

10 basil leaves, torn

2 mint leaves, finely sliced

8 sprigs fresh marjoram, leaves removed and stalks discarded

Dressing

2 small tomatoes

¼ cup olive oil

1 tablespoon red wine vinegar

½ tablespoon balsamic vinegar

2 cloves garlic

salt and freshly ground black pepper

1 Preheat oven to 200ºC (180ºC fan, 400ºF, gas 6). Cut the bread into cubes and toss with olive oil and rosemary. Spread out on a baking tray (sheet) and bake for 5 minutes until golden, then cool.

2 To make the dressing, heat a heavy pan and brush the skins of the small tomatoes with a little olive oil. Cook these whole tomatoes in the pan until well blackened all over. Purée with the remaining olive oil, vinegars, garlic and salt and pepper to taste. Set aside.

3 Remove the seeds from the other tomatoes and chop the flesh into small chunks. Peel the cucumber and remove the seeds by running a teaspoon along the central seed area. Slice finely. Remove the stones from the olives by squashing them with the wide blade of a knife.

4 In a mixing bowl, place the bread cubes, tomatoes, cucumber, onion, olives and basil leaves. Add the chopped mint and marjoram. Mix well. Pour the dressing over and toss thoroughly. Allow to sit for 10 minutes then serve.

Pila di Melanzana

Serves 4 · Preparation and cooking 40 minutes

¼ cup olive oil

2 large eggplants (aubergines)

1 red capsicum (pepper), quartered

4 Roma tomatoes, sliced

freshly ground black pepper

4 bocconcini, sliced

¼ cup basil leaves

pinch of sea salt

Balsamic dressing

¼ cup olive oil

2 tablespoons balsamic vinegar

1 Preheat the oven to 150°C (130°C fan, 300°F, gas 2).

2 Heat a chargrill (char-broil) pan and brush lightly with oil. Slice each of the eggplants (aubergines) into 8 slices about 15mm (½in) thick, brush with oil and chargrill 2–3 minutes each side. Place capsicum (pepper) under a hot griller (broiler) and cook until skin is black. Remove skin and discard, then finely slice capsicum flesh.

3 Brush tomato slices with oil, sprinkle with pepper, place on a lightly oiled baking tray (sheet) and roast for 15 minutes. Add the eggplant pieces and cook for a further 10 minutes.

4 On a serving plate, place 2 slices of eggplant, top with 3 strips of capsicum, 3 slices of tomato, 3 slices of bocconcini and 2 more strips of capsicum. Garnish with basil leaves.

5 Combine the dressing ingredients. Drizzle balsamic dressing over dish and top with a good grind of sea salt and black pepper just before serving. Serve with crusty Italian bread.

Roasted Beetroot, Orange and Fennel Salad

Serves 4 · Preparation and cooking 1 hour 30 minutes

3 large beetroots

2 teaspoons brown sugar

1 teaspoon salt

2 sprigs fresh rosemary, leaves removed and chopped

2 tablespoons olive oil

1 bulb fennel

2 blood oranges

100g (3½oz) toasted hazelnuts, crushed

Dressing

½ bunch dill (dill weed), chopped

2 tablespoons balsamic vinegar

½ cup olive oil

salt and freshly ground black pepper

1 Preheat the oven to 180°C (160°C fan, 350°F, gas 4). Wash and trim the beetroots at root and stem ends but do not peel.

2 In a small bowl, mix together the brown sugar, salt, rosemary and oil until well blended then add the whole beetroots and toss in the oil mixture, making sure that the beetroot skins are all shiny. Wrap each beetroot in foil, place in a baking dish, then roast for approximately 1 hour or until just tender. Peel the beetroots and cut into thick slices.

3 Very finely slice the fennel bulb and peel the oranges, trimming any pith. Cut the orange into segments.

4 To make the dressing, combine the dill (dill weed), balsamic vinegar, olive oil, salt and pepper and whisk until thick.

5 Arrange the beetroots on a serving platter with the fennel and orange. Drizzle over the dressing then scatter the crushed hazelnuts on top.

Pakistani Green Bean Salad

Serves 4–6 · Preparation and cooking 25 minutes

750g (1½lb) fresh green (string) beans

25mm (1in) piece fresh ginger (gingerroot)

1 tablespoon vegetable oil

1 tablespoon sesame oil

1 teaspoon mustard seeds

2 teaspoons ground cumin

½ teaspoon ground turmeric

1 fresh green chilli, finely minced

150ml (5fl oz) chicken or vegetable stock (broth)

juice of 2 lemons

1 bunch fresh coriander (cilantro), washed, dried then chopped

pinch of salt

90g (3oz) peanuts, roasted and chopped

1   Trim the beans and discard any discoloured ends. Peel the ginger (gingerroot) and cut into fine matchsticks.

2   Heat a wok with the vegetable and sesame oils and, when hot, add the mustard seeds. Allow them to cook for a moment or two until they start popping. Add the ginger and cook for a further minute. Add the ground cumin, turmeric and chilli and stir until fragrant, about 2 minutes.

3   Add all the beans and toss in the flavoured oil to coat them thoroughly. Add the stock (broth), cover and simmer for 5–8 minutes or until the liquid has almost evaporated completely and the beans are tender.

4   Remove the lid and add the lemon juice, coriander (cilantro) and salt to taste. Stir thoroughly to combine all the ingredients then cool. Serve garnished with roasted chopped peanuts and, if desired, lemon wedges.

Sweet Potato and Peanut Salad

Serves 8 as a side dish · Preparation and cooking 1 hour 40 minutes

1¾kg (4lb) sweet potato (yam), peeled

6 tablespoons olive oil

20 cloves garlic, unpeeled

salt and freshly ground black pepper

1 red onion, ground

1–2 small red chillies, ground

½ cup fresh herbs such as coriander (cilantro), parsley, dill (dill weed), chives or a mixture

2 tablespoons balsamic vinegar

2 cups roasted peanuts

1 Preheat oven to 220°C (200°C fan, 430°F, gas 7). Cut the sweet potato (yam) into large chunks. Toss with 2 tablespoons of the oil and place in a large baking dish with the garlic. Season with salt and pepper and bake for about 1 hour or until the sweet potato is tender and golden around the edges. Remove from the oven and keep warm.

2 Mix the onion and chilli with the fresh herbs and combine with the sweet potato. Whisk the remaining olive oil with the vinegar and toss with the sweet potato mixture. Add the peanuts, toss again and serve garnished with extra herb sprigs.

Asian Gingered Coleslaw

Serves 6 · Preparation 30 minutes

½ large curly cabbage, very finely sliced, about 5 cups

4 baby bok choy, leaves separated and sliced

8 spring (green) onions, julienned

200g (7oz) canned sliced water chestnuts, drained

2 medium carrots, finely julienned

2 stalks lemongrass, finely sliced

4 kaffir lime leaves, finely sliced

Dressing

2 tablespoons mayonnaise

2 tablespoons natural yoghurt

juice of 2 lemons

juice of 1 lime

5cm (2in) piece ginger (gingerroot), grated

4 tablespoons rice vinegar

salt and freshly ground black pepper

Garnish

1 bunch coriander (cilantro), roughly chopped

½ cup toasted peanuts or sunflower seeds

1 Finely slice the cabbage and mix in a large bowl with the sliced bok choy, green onions, water chestnuts, carrots and finely sliced lemongrass and lime leaves. Toss thoroughly.

2 In a jug, whisk together all the dressing ingredients until smooth and well seasoned then pour over the salad ingredients and toss thoroughly until all the vegetables are coated with the dressing.

3 To serve, mix through the coriander (cilantro) at the last minute and sprinkle with the peanuts or sunflower seeds.

Warm Tomato Gratin Salad

Serves 4 · Preparation and cooking 30 minutes

30g (1oz) butter, melted

4 tablespoons olive oil

2 cups fresh breadcrumbs

½ cup parsley, chopped

20 large basil leaves, finely sliced

½ bunch chives, chopped

salt and freshly ground black pepper

6–8 large tomatoes

200g (7oz) assorted mixed lettuce leaves

1 tablespoon balsamic vinegar

1 Preheat oven to 180ºC (160ºC fan, 350ºF, gas 4). Heat the butter and half the olive oil in a large frying pan (skillet) and add the breadcrumbs, parsley, basil and chives and toss until golden. Add salt and pepper to taste.

2 Thickly slice the tomatoes and place them on a non-stick baking tray (sheet), adding salt and pepper to taste, then press the crumb mixture over the tomatoes to cover each slice.

3 Bake the tomatoes for 10 minutes, then grill (broil) just to toast the crumbs.

4 Meanwhile, toss the lettuce leaves with the combined remaining olive oil and vinegar and add salt and pepper to taste.

5 Arrange the lettuce leaves on a platter then top with the tomato slices, allowing each to overlap the previous one. Grind black pepper over and serve.

Gingered Almond Broccoli Salad with Cellophane Noodles

Serves 6–8 · Preparation and cooking 30 minutes

1 tablespoon peanut oil

5cm (2in) piece fresh ginger (gingerroot), grated

1 small hot red chilli, very finely sliced

4 cloves garlic, minced

4 spring (green) onions, sliced

500g (1lb) broccoli florets, trimmed

10 fresh shiitake mushrooms, sliced

200g (7oz) baby corn

3 tablespoons soy sauce

3 tablespoons mirin

2 tablespoons rice vinegar

1 cos (romaine) lettuce, shredded

125g (4oz) blanched almonds, toasted

Noodles

100g (3½oz) dried cellophane noodles

2 tablespoons fish sauce

2 tablespoons rice vinegar

2 tablespoons mirin

1 teaspoon palm or brown sugar

½ cup fresh coriander (cilantro), chopped

1   First, prepare the noodles. Fill a deep jug or bowl with very warm water and soak the cellophane noodles for about 10 minutes or until they are soft and tender. Drain. Mix together the fish sauce, rice vinegar, mirin and sugar then toss through the cellophane noodles. Add the coriander (cilantro), mix well and set aside.

2   Heat the peanut oil in a wok and add the ginger (gingerroot), chilli, garlic and spring (green) onions and toss thoroughly until the spring onions have wilted, about 3 minutes.

3   Add the broccoli florets and toss well until bright green. Add the mushrooms and corn and continue tossing over a high heat. Add the soy, mirin and rice vinegar and continue cooking for 1 minute.

4   Add the noodles and mix well then remove the pan from the heat.

5   Divide the shredded lettuce amongst the serving plates then top with the broccoli noodle mixture. Garnish with toasted almonds and extra chopped coriander.

Celeriac and Herb Remoulade

Serves 4 · Preparation and cooking 30 minutes

2 medium eggs

500g (1lb) celeriac, grated

2 tablespoons olive oil

1 tablespoon sesame oil

juice of 1 lemon

¼ cup fresh parsley, chopped

½ small bunch fresh chives, chopped

salt and freshly ground black pepper

1 Bring a saucepan of water to the boil. Add the eggs and boil for 10 minutes. Cool under cold running water, then remove the shells and finely chop the eggs.

2 Place the celeriac and chopped eggs in a large bowl. Mix together the olive oil, sesame oil and lemon juice and pour over the celeriac and eggs. Add the parsley, chives and seasoning, then mix thoroughly.

Sicilian Cauliflower Salad

Serves 4 · Preparation and cooking 40 minutes + 1 hour cooling

1 small cauliflower

30g (1oz) seedless raisins (dark raisins)

1 tablespoon toasted flaked almonds

grated zest of 1 small lemon

¼ cup fresh flat-leaf parsley, chopped

Dressing

juice of 1 small lemon

½ teaspoon ground cinnamon

pinch of cayenne pepper

5 tablespoons extra virgin olive oil

2 teaspoons balsamic vinegar

1 teaspoon caster (berry) sugar

salt and freshly ground black pepper

1 Cut the cauliflower into small florets and slice the stalk into bite-size pieces. Cook in lightly salted boiling water for 2–3 minutes until softened but still firm to the bite. Drain well.

2 To make the dressing, place the lemon juice in a screw-top jar with the cinnamon, cayenne, oil, vinegar, sugar and seasoning and shake well, or place the ingredients in a bowl and mix with a fork. Pour the dressing over the cauliflower and toss to coat. Leave to cool for 1 hour.

3 Meanwhile, pour enough boiling water over the raisins to cover, then leave for 10 minutes to plump up. Drain and chop roughly. Scatter over the cauliflower with the almonds, lemon zest and parsley and toss lightly.

Fruit

A fruit salad is a refreshing and healthy
dessert, while recipes such as Waldorf Salad
or Fruit and Nut Salad are tasty main course
accompaniments, which bring a welcome
hint of sweetness to savoury dishes.

Waldorf Salad

Serves 4 · Preparation 5 minutes

1 green apple, cut into chunks

1 red apple, cut into chunks

1 stalk (rib) celery, sliced

5 baby cos (romaine) leaves, finely shredded

¼ cup mayonnaise

1 teaspoon lemon juice

¼ cup pecan or walnut halves

1 Combine the apples, celery and lettuce in a bowl with the mayonnaise, lemon juice and pecans or walnuts.

2 Mix well and serve.

Fruit and Nut Salad

Serves 4 · Preparation 8 minutes

2 red apples, chopped

2 stalks (ribs) celery, sliced

250g (8oz) strawberries, halved

3 tablespoons sultanas (golden raisins)

60g (2oz) chopped pecans

Dressing

4 sprigs fresh mint, finely chopped

3 tablespoons natural yoghurt

2 tablespoons lemon juice

freshly ground black pepper

1 Place apples, celery, strawberries, sultanas (golden raisins) and pecans in a salad bowl.

2 To make dressing, place mint, yoghurt, lemon juice and black pepper to taste in a bowl and stir to combine.

3 Spoon the dressing over the salad and toss to combine. Cover and refrigerate until required.

Fresh Fruit Salad

Serves 4 · Preparation 20 minutes + 1 hour chilling

2 oranges

2–3 tablespoons fresh, unsweetened orange juice

1 red apple, cored but not peeled, cut into 1cm (½in) pieces

1 pear, cored, peeled and cut into 1cm (½in) pieces

60g (2oz) seedless grapes

1 ripe nectarine, skinned, stoned and cut into chunks

1 banana

6 strawberries

½ cup natural yoghurt

1 Slice the top and bottom off each orange and place on a work surface. Using a serrated knife, cut off the skin and pith, following the curve of the fruit. Holding the oranges over a bowl, cut between the membranes to release the segments. Put the segments into a large serving bowl with the orange juice.

2 Add the apple, pear, grapes and nectarine to the bowl and mix gently but thoroughly so that the orange juice coats the fruit (this will stop the fruit discolouring). Put the fruit salad in the refrigerator and chill for 1 hour to allow the flavours to develop.

3 Just before serving, peel the banana, slice thinly and add to the bowl. Remove the green hulls from the strawberries, cut in half and add to the bowl. Mix gently and divide between 4 serving bowls. Top each with yoghurt and serve.

Citrus Fruit Salad with Ginger

Serves 4 · Preparation and cooking 30 minutes

1 pink grapefruit

1 large orange

1 tangerine, peeled and divided into segments

zest of 1 lime, cut into matchsticks

60g (2oz) kumquats, halved, pips removed

juice of 1 small lemon

150ml (5fl oz) ginger beer

3 tablespoons caster (berry) sugar

2 pieces preserved ginger in syrup, finely chopped

fresh mint leaves

1 Slice the tops and bottoms off the grapefruit and orange using a sharp serrated knife – hold the fruit over a bowl to catch the juices. Cut down the side of the fruits, following the curves, to remove the skin and pith. Cut out the segments, leaving the membranes behind. Place in a serving dish with the tangerine segments. Reserve the fruit juices.

2 Place the lime zest and kumquats in a saucepan with 150ml (5fl oz) water. Simmer for 10 minutes or until softened. Add the kumquats to the other fruit and drain the lime zest on absorbent paper. Reserve the liquid.

3 Add the lemon juice, ginger beer, sugar and any juices from the fruit to the reserved cooking liquid. Heat gently, stirring, for 5 minutes or until the sugar dissolves. Pour the mixture over the fruit and stir in the chopped ginger. Sprinkle over the lime zest and garnish with fresh mint.

Oriental Fruit Salad

Serves 4 · Preparation and cooking 20 minutes + 30 minutes chilling

3 stalks lemongrass

60g (2oz) caster (berry) sugar

1 small rockmelon (canteloupe)

1 mango

400g (14oz) canned lychees, drained

fresh mint leaves

1　Peel outer layers from lemongrass stalks, finely chop lower white bulbous parts and discard fibrous tops. Place lemongrass, sugar and 100ml (4fl oz) water in a saucepan. Simmer, stirring, for 5 minutes or until the sugar dissolves, then bring to the boil. Remove from the heat and leave to cool for 20 minutes. Refrigerate for 30 minutes.

2　Halve melon and scrape out seeds. Cut into wedges, then remove skin and cut flesh into small chunks. Slice off the 2 fat sides of the mango close to the stone. Cut a criss-cross pattern across the flesh (but not through the skin) of each piece, then push the skin inside out to expose the cubes of flesh and cut them off.

3　Place melon, mango and lychees in serving bowls. Strain lemongrass syrup and pour over the fruit. Garnish with mint and serve.

Fruit Salad in Spicy Lime Syrup

Serves 4 · Preparation and cooking 15 minutes

½ pineapple, diced

1 mango, diced

1 papaya, diced

1 apple, cored and diced

1 continental (English) cucumber, peeled and diced

12 rambutans, peeled and deseeded

Syrup

1 cup brown sugar

grated zest of 1 lime

2 tablespoons lime juice

1 teaspoon tamarind paste

1 medium-sized chilli, deseeded and finely chopped

1 To make syrup, combine sugar, lime zest and juice with ½ cup water in a small saucepan. Bring to the boil and simmer over low heat for 8–10 minutes. Allow to cool. Add tamarind paste and chilli and stir to combine.

2 Combine fruit in a serving bowl. Pour over syrup and toss before serving.

Weights and Measures

Weights and measures differ from country to country, but with these handy conversion charts cooking has never been easier!

Cup Measurements

One cup of these commonly used ingredients is equal to the following weights.

Ingredient	Metric	Imperial
Apples (dried and chopped)	125g	4½oz
Apricots (dried and chopped)	190g	6¾oz
Breadcrumbs (packet)	125g	4½oz
Breadcrumbs (soft)	55g	2oz
Butter	225g	8oz
Cheese (shredded/grated)	115g	4oz
Choc bits	155g	5½oz
Coconut (desiccated/fine)	90g	3oz
Flour (plain/all-purpose, self-raising)	115g	4oz
Fruit (dried)	170g	6oz
Golden (corn) syrup	315g	11oz
Honey	315g	11oz
Margarine	225g	8oz
Nuts (chopped)	115g	4oz
Rice (cooked)	155g	5½oz
Rice (uncooked)	225g	8oz
Sugar (brown)	155g	5½oz
Sugar (caster/berry/superfine)	225g	8oz
Sugar (granulated)	225g	8oz
Sugar (sifted, icing/confectioner's)	155g	5½oz
Treacle (molasses)	315g	11oz

Oven Temperatures

Celsius	Fahrenheit	Gas mark
120	250	1
150	300	2
160	320	3
180	350	4
190	375	5
200	400	6
220	430	7
230	450	8
250	480	9

Liquid Measures

Cup	Metric	Imperial
¼ cup	63ml	2¼fl oz
½ cup	125ml	4½fl oz
¾ cup	188ml	6⅔fl oz
1 cup	250ml	8¾fl oz
1¾ cup	438ml	15½fl oz
2 cups	500ml	17½fl oz
4 cups	1 litre	35fl oz

Spoon	Metric	Imperial
¼ teaspoon	1.25ml	1/25fl oz
½ teaspoon	2.5ml	1/12fl oz
1 teaspoon	5ml	⅙fl oz
1 tablespoon	15ml	½fl oz

Weight Measures

Metric	Imperial
10g	¼oz
15g	½oz
20g	¾oz
30g	1oz
60g	2oz
115g	4oz (¼lb)
125g	4½oz
145g	5oz
170g	6oz
185g	6½oz
200g	7oz
225g	8oz (½lb)
300g	10½oz
330g	11½oz
370g	13oz
400g	14oz
425g	15oz
455g	16oz (1lb)
500g	17½oz (1lb 1½oz)
600g	21oz (1lb 5oz)
650g	23oz (1lb 7oz)
750g	26½oz (1lb 10½oz)
1000g (1kg)	35oz (2lb 3oz)

Index